Intimacy

REDEMPTION *from* PERVERSION

BISHOP
HAROLD GENTRY

WESTBOW
PRESS®
A DIVISION OF THOMAS NELSON
& ZONDERVAN

WestBow Press books may be ordered through booksellers or by contacting:

WestBow Press
A Division of Thomas Nelson & Zondervan
1663 Liberty Drive
Bloomington, IN 47403
www.westbowpress.com
844-714-3454

ISBN: 978-1-6642-1233-6 (sc)
ISBN: 978-1-6642-1234-3 (hc)
ISBN: 978-1-6642-1232-9 (e)

Library of Congress Control Number: 2020922686

Print information available on the last page.

WestBow Press rev. date: 01/20/2021

CONTENTS

*"The Weight of a Gift is Measured
by Living It's Purpose"*

Harold Gentry

PREFACE

It is a delight and an honor for me that Bishop Gentry, my dear friend, has asked me to share this portion of his book as the preface. I said to him after reading halfway through this great piece of work, "Please do not donate a copy to me but allow me to pay for the cost of the book". I could not allow such a gift to be given without an offering on my part expressing my appreciation for his hard work. The book is done with such passion and power as he takes his artful time in laying out the case of such a needed tool for ministering and necessary instrument for every serious counselor though secular or Christian. Each chapter could be used in pre- marriage counseling sessions and minister to couples who are experiencing some deficiency in their relationship. Allow me to lift just a snippet of what you will behold in this presentation. "There is nothing X-Rated between the Christian husband and wife's sexual activities and discussions". Your words should speak loud and descriptive while your body is complimenting what you have spoken. Both husband and wife should honor God in maintaining the pulchritude (physical beauty; comeliness) that He made and gave when he formed man". Well, there is much more as he shares subjects like body language, the language of sex, it is ministry with potent craftsmanship. I was moved to even a deeper love and appreciation for my own spouse as I journeyed from chapter to chapter. This body of work will be added to my counseling profile and counseling classes. Every pastor needs this piece of literature not merely for the bookshelf to add with one's collection but rather on the desk as a must read. The honesty, openness, conversational, revelations in such an efficacious way of handling each chapter is a testament to the energy, prayer, and labor Bishop Gentry has spent in delivering such a wonderful work. Thank you, my friend, for writing with a sense of divine urgency and mandate in sharing this with not just the body of Christ but with everyone who desires a healthy relationship and a wholesome marriage. I have been moved by this amazing feat.

Blessings and Peace,

++Larry Donnell Jones-Leonard Sr
Presiding Prelate of New Covenant Churches International

++LDonnellLeonardSr

INTRODUCTION

"If there's a book that you want to read, but it hasn't been written yet, you must be the one to write it".

—Toni Morrison

I want to share with the body of Christ and others who will read this book some truths that are untaught and maybe to some degree, unknown. I believe the position the Body of Christ and His church has taken on sex is due to the lack of understanding of the original intent and God-given purpose.

> *"For we are members of His body, of His flesh and His bones. "For this reason a man shall leave his father and mother and be joined to his wife, and the two shall become one flesh". This is a great mystery, but I speak concerning Christ and the church".* (Ephesians 5:30–32)

It is a mystery while reasoning with God as we travel toward the revelation of purpose. All through the Word of God, God is trying to get us to see things from His point of reference and not of the mind of man. I know that you, as a Bible scholar, have already gone to Isaiah 1:18 where God says to us, "Come now, and let us reason together," The word *reason* in the Hebrew expression is saying to us, "Let Me (God) argue with you, as you pray and meditate, see that I am right in all that I say, what I am saying, and what I have said, proving to you that I am (God) is right." Isaiah 1:10 says, "Hear the word of the Lord, You rulers of Sodom; Give ear to the law of our God, you people of Gomorrah". Isaiah 1:18 is not saying, take our finite mind with limited knowledge to think and reason with any thought or plan to change the mind of God. Paul reminds us:

> *"Let no one deceive himself. If anyone among you seems to be wise in this age, let him become a fool that he may become wise. For the wisdom of this world is foolishness with God. For it is written, He catches the wise in their own craftinessand again, The Lord knows the thoughts of the wise, that they are futile".*
> (1 Corinthians 3:18-20)

When God made man, He started the relationship with intimacy, *"image and likeness"*. That level of intimacy is spiritual that God Himself chooses to manage. The truest intimacy between a husband and wife is when God reveals to each of them, substance of His nature of love embedded in each for the other. These are God's personal gifts of delight, glee, and character, experienced only by those whom He has joined together. This type of God purposed intimacy creates a bond that incites a worship in all segments of the marital relationship.

It is a bonding fashioned by the spirit of God and welcomed by the man and woman.

> "And Adam said, "This is now bone of my bones and flesh of my flesh; She shall be called Woman, Because she was taken out of Man" (Genesis 2:23).

The revelation that came to Adam from the substance God embedded in him, gives birth to Genesis 2:24.

> "Therefore a man shall leave his father and mother and be joined to his wife, and they shall become one flesh".

The goal of intimacy is to develop a comfort of trust and assurance of a forever being one until the agent of death occur. I pray that as you read this book you would open your mind to see, by revelation, God's word and not any preconceived thoughts that may be planted in your mind by misconception and possibly your thoughts. I know that as you read, you and your mate's life with God will spiral to another level of clarity and freedom. And for you, that are parents, will engage in Holy reverence and understanding to give you comfort in teaching your children about their bodies and God's plan and purpose for sex. If you have not confessed a faith in Jesus Christ, I believe that as you read this book the Holy Spirit will awaken your mind and spirit to see the need to have Jesus Christ as your redeemer, helper, comforter, and a genuine friend for life. As you read, you will conceive and fully understand all that God has for you as it relates to you as a husband or wife in your relationship with each other. I trust the Holy Spirit will comfort you as He uncovers truths lined in the reading.

> Truth is not a common map for every life, but a SEED to develop directions for each individual life through a prescribed path.

CHAPTER ONE

THE BOND BEFORE THE BONDING

W HEN LIVING IN the spirit realm of God's order, there is a oneness of completeness without any error. Can you imagine a life without needing any corrections with steps of progressions and experiencing a perfect relationship with God and your mate? Before we can properly think or envision a perfect relationship, we must see God as God before experiencing earthly thinking, events, schedules, and even accomplishments. A realization of God before the creation of man can birth a respect for Him beyond any human expressions. Phillip Keller, the author of "R*abboni*" said, "We must envisage the endless eons of eternity. Somehow, we must grasp with the deep intuition of our spirits the realm of the supernatural, where time and space and our physical senses are no longer the basis of our observations".

Even with the immense mind that God gave to mankind, it is impossible to fully explain God and His existence, so please allow me to use a statement that I say in some occasions as I minister, "The Always Been and the IS God." As you read this book, I will, with my finite mind, use other phrases attempting to express my mind and heart's understanding and expressions about God and the things He has done and put in place for man before man was created and made. In my mind and life, I am constantly reminding myself of God being completely informed of everything about man and the needs of man. It is comforting to not only imagine but to know that every molecule, every micro part of my body, every concept of my being is only a mere fraction of the mind of God. And yet He has complete knowledge of everything I need in the total existence of my life, and not only me but every created being. Not only is He fully knowledgeable of me, but all that He is exist in the smallest micro cell of my existence. So, there is nothing of you and I He does not know. In His love for us, He has structured for us to have complete fulfillment in every concept of our lives. Therefore, we should praise and thank Him at every thought of Him. Abraham Heschel, the author of, *Man Is Not Alone*, said, "Unless we know how to praise Him, we can't learn how to know Him".

Now, let us study this thought. We know that He is the eternal God, an infinite God, an all-knowing God, and He is beyond all that we could imagine or think. He is God, who is incapable of making a mistake. He cannot have an ungodly thought, and everything of Him and about Him is conclusive. What He is, is what He was, and What He is to become is what He has been. The question must be asked with a respectful attempt to answer, how can we as humans have a relationship with eternity? A relationship is more than just an acquaintance or an announcement of a position. It is a state of being connected, it is an interconnected behavior where each reflects the other. How can infinite fellowship with finite? How can the eternal have a relationship with that which has a beginning? It stands to reason that we must simply trust and believe what God has spoken and He can do whatever He desires and chooses without any accusation or fact of error. It is the unexplainable truth that we as believers are entwined by Jesus Christ with an infinite God, yet He is independent of us by the blood of Jesus to maintain His Holiness.

> *Then God said, "Let Us make man in Our image, according to Our likeness; let them have dominion over the fish of the sea, over the birds of the air, and over the cattle, over all the earth and over every creeping thing that creeps on the earth." So, God created man in His own image; in the image of God He created him; male and female He created them* (Genesis 1:26–27).

It is God and God alone who made man and structured him to have a relationship with the eternal. He put in man what is necessary for that relationship. What caused God to create and make a man? Was there a need? What was the reason? There is always a reason for God to do anything, but His reasons are not easily ascertained. One thing God leaves us with to know and cherish is, His love is always the essence of what he does.

The poem *"Creation"* by James Weldon Johnson, speaks of God creating all things. One section from his poem speaks of God's reason for creating man.

Then God walked around,
And God looked around
On all that He had made.
He looked at His moon,
And He looked at His little stars;
He looked on His world
With all its living things,
And God said, *"I am lonely still."*

Then God sat down—
On the side of a hill where he could think
By a deep, wide river he sat down;
With his head in his hands,
God thought and thought,
Till he thought, *"I'll make me a man!"*

I will never discredit the awesome thoughts, the creativity, and the originality of a world-renowned poem, I will only add a truth from the word of God.

"He who does not love does not know God, <u>for God is love</u>" (1 John 4:8).

In speaking of love, it is fully giving all of self. Love is a single force that caused God to bring forth everything. Love is the only source of strength that crushes hatred and prejudice and releases genuine building blocks of allegiant brotherhood and fellowship. Love says "I will" without referencing a magnitude of any difficulty. Love is an attribute that insists on sharing. God said, "Let Us make man in Our image, according to Our likeness";

If you notice, He did not establish any limitations on what He said. What is this that God is making and fashioning as He? It is the spirit of man that is now created and made in the image and likeness of God. It is that part of man that isn't seen until manifested through actions and deeds. The body of man that was formed around the spirit of man was necessary to function as physical living.

"And the Lord God formed man of the dust of the ground and breathed into his nostrils the breath of life; and man became a living being" (Genesis 2:7).

God formed man from the substance of the earth, the dust of the ground wrapped around the spirit of man, made it legal for God in man to operate in the earth realm. God put in man everything necessary to function as God in the earth realm, yet man can enjoy life as a human being. It is human flesh surrounding the image of God which He called man. It was God's intention for everything that mankind does, and experience, would reflect God in all that He is. Because of love, God could not create something that could not love as well. Man can love as God loves. And because of that, one element of the man's being that God, because He is love, gave to man is a free-will. It is the only thing God gave to man that God Himself will not touch. God's love demands for us to have freedom of choice. God did not make us with a demand or a must to love Him. He made us with a choice to love Him. Flowing in a bond of love produces godly functioning as God. The pure love of God in the spirit of man functions with the true nature of uncontaminated trust. Pure love must leave us with a choice so that trust can be proven. The only way trust can be proven is to have options to choose to obey or not to obey. Adam lived in a bond with God, not in bondage to God. My expression of what I understand God is saying to Adam, "As I expose and give my Love to you, I must also show you that I choose to trust you to maintain My image and My likeness in you." God's bond of love gave to Adam and all of mankind a free will to be or not to be.

Now that man lives in what I call, an earth suit, that suit must live from the substance he was formed from.

> *"The Lord God planted a garden eastward in Eden, and there He put the man whom He had formed"* (Genesis 2:8).

> *"Then the Lord God took the man and put him in the garden of Eden to tend and keep it"* (Genesis 2:15).

All that God made must have God to continue to exist with God being the source. *"He himself is before all things and all things are held together in him"* (Colossians 1:17, NET). The state of the existence of all God made depended on Adam's tending and keeping. In Genesis 2:15, The word -tend- in the New King James Version, and the word -dress- in the King James Version is the Hebrew word, -abad- meaning to work, to serve, and to worship. The Hebrew word for -keep- is shamar---meaning to guard, to protect, be secured, observe. With God, there is always an order to how all things are to function and maintained in their existence. All the while Adam was to keep or tend, there was always an expectancy to give God praise and maintain a worship atmosphere. He was to maintain and keep everything of God's creation in the order that was given. Even Adam was to maintain himself as to how God made Him. How much God loved Adam was never a question, but it is how much and how well did Adam love God? Adam's love had to be tested and proven. Love does not love if the one who is loved is controlled and forced to function without a choice. In that God is love, He allowed Adam to have choices. Even with choices, it was still Adam's responsibility to maintain the state of being of creation and to always present things to God as God presented them to him. Even after Eve was brought to Adam, Adam was still responsible for maintaining the state of being of God's creation.

This bond of pure love and trust, in the basic sense, lived in God's statement to Adam, all that I have made will be whatever you call it.

> *"Out of the ground the Lord God formed every beast of the field and every bird of the air and brought them to Adam to see what he would call them. And whatever Adam called each living creature, that was its name"* (Genesis 2:19).

It is extremely difficult to destroy a relationship when oneness is lived. Adam and Eve had the privilege of being one with God before living together as one. It is living in the earth realm together with the same understanding and acceptance, respecting our origin of existence. They were one in Adam before the two became one with Him.

"So God created man in His own image; in the image of God He created him; male and female He created them" (Genesis 1:27).

Only God can answer how male and female existed in Adam until He removed a rib from Adam and made Eve, the woman. So, there was already a oneness of male and female to be one with each other and one in God.

And Adam said: "This is now bone of my bones and flesh of my flesh; She shall be called Woman because she was taken out of Man" (Genesis 2:23).

There will forever be a pang of hunger and love in God's heart for oneness with man whom He created.

I watched a movie once, where this young girl was impregnated at a young age and knowing the improbabilities to properly provide for the child, she gave the child up for adoption. Over the years of her life, she could never extirpate from her heart the longing for the oneness of the life that had lived in her for nine months. As I watched the movie unfold, I sensed the longing of God's heart for the fellowship and interactions with all He made and His created beings. Not only to be one with Him and to express the praise and worship of our hearts to Him, but also the loving and caring for us He longs to give.

God structured the nature and soundness of relationships to evolve from our oneness with Him. When there is oneness with God, there is living within us to have a constant thought of thankfulness, a cohesiveness of cooperation, an atmosphere of worship, and a devotion of pleasing Him, our Creator. While we are participating in a divine prerequisite and heavenly expectancy of praise and worship, God our Creator is preparing what we need before the need becomes apparent to us. Simply said, "As we participate in His kingdom functions and agenda, it is His responsibility to supply all and everything that we need".

As you continue to read, I pray you will see the truths that God gave to us before the fall of man, in Genesis 3. When these truths are revealed and accepted, Satan will be robbed of his strength of deception, spiritual delusions, and perversion that is so destructive among mankind today. You will see the nature of Satan's envy, and anger at God and man. Satan saw that God gave to man something far greater than his existence could ever fathom. I pray that by the time you finish reading this book, you will repent, as I did, for taking for granted the true immensity God gave to mankind in the relationship of husband and wife.

"For in Him dwells all the fullness of the Godhead bodily; and you are complete in Him, who is the head of all principality and power" (Colossians 2:9–10).

CHAPTER TWO

THE ORIGIN OF INTIMACY

THERE HAS BEEN so much said and thoughts expressed about sex that are wrong, misunderstood, and misleading that even Christians are confused. If God called everything He made *"very good"*, that is inclusive of gifts God gave to man as well. So, where did the misconception begin? In *"The Biblical Perspective"*, Charles Phillips wrote,

> "The Church's attitude about sex goes back hundreds of years to one great theologian, St. Augustine, who had a strong influence on the Church in his day. I believe his viewpoints are one of the major reasons the Church views sex as it does today".

I agree with Charles Phillips.

St. Augustine was a great theologian and scholar, who did some tremendous things as it relates to bringing revelation and insight to the scriptures. In Lester Sumrall's book, *"60 Things God Said About Sex"*, he said that St. Augustine's position on sexual matters was rather basic and disdaining. He also reported several additional statements:

1. He believed that sex was sinful. He believed that Adam and Eve's problem in the Garden of Eden was because of sex.
2. He believed eating the 'forbidden fruit' represented sex.
3. He thought Eve conceived and bore children in pain (Genesis 3:16) because sex is sinful, and any kind of sexual activity brings pain.
4. Human beings should ask God's forgiveness for even thinking about sex and should abstain whenever possible.
5. Men and women who want to be righteous in God's sight should live in celibacy.

The obvious realization is, St. Augustine never said, the Holy Spirit said to him, but he said he believed. I once believed that speaking in tongues was made up of those who spoke in tongues until it happened to me. When I was filled with the Holy Spirit, the experience of speaking in other tongues came upon me and I spoke as the Spirit gave me utterance. Thank God that He is still being patient with us until we come into the knowledge of true revelation. Because St. Augustine is no longer living in the flesh, I cannot pray for him, but I can pray for those who are still affected by the misconception that sex should be abstained from our thinking whenever possible.

If the statement originated from God, God contradicted Himself. One thing that I have learned as I study God's Word is to take all the time needed for God to speak to me in His Word and from His word. In other words, you cannot read in a hurry.

To just read the Word of God, I will know what I read, but it is very possible not to hear what God is saying. In the study of God's Word, it is necessary to hear the heart of God. I desire to know how and what God is thinking and the present intention of His heart in His words. We have had the Bible for thousands of years, yet God is still saying what He said and yet speaking in the now. Even though it was written many years ago, it is still relevant today, because God is omniscient. The Holy Spirit can still cause our mind and spirit to be sagacious enough that we can hear what He is saying to us in the now. As we study, it is not just learning what is said but a fellowshipping and discussing with the writer. Let us investigate the Word of God to know truth in all cases.

> *Then God blessed them, and God said to them, "Be fruitful and multiply; fill the earth and subdue it; have dominion over the fish of the sea, over the birds of the air, and over every living thing that moves on the earth"* (Genesis 1:28).

God blessed (Barak) them. God, Himself showed them adoration, and His instruction to them was to be fruitful and multiply. The Oxford Dictionary defines fruitful as producing good or helpful results. The Hebrew word, *parah*, is to bear fruit. God was not only releasing instructions but also permission. God made man, the spirit of man and the physical man, therefore He knows the total concept of what the man needs. The origin of their fulfillment comes from the source of origination. When God blessed them, He released to them total fulfillment. Be all that I am in you and to one another. Although the woman was taken from the body of the man that was to be formed, God had already set in place the fulness of function and fulfillment. When God said, "*be fruitful*" He was also giving and permitting them to experience the fullness one to the other. God is God, and we, as finite, can never experience the total completeness of God. But each day of our existence, we can experience a greater and growing sense of the enactment of His person. That is why each encounter of the sexual experience of husband and wife can never be duplicated. Each experience is new and fresh. Again, according to St. Augustine, "Human beings should ask God's forgiveness for even thinking about sex and should abstain whenever possible". The question I must leave with you, how can "*Be fruitful and multiply*" be also evil or punishment?

Now come with me and let us go further into the mind of God. In Genesis 2, God is now forming man, giving him a body. He also made the body with its needs, and the ability to complete His assignment of multiplying and replenishing the earth.

> "*And the Lord God said, "It is not good that man should be alone; I will make him a helper comparable to him. Out of the ground, the Lord God formed every beast of the field and every bird of the air and* **brought** *them to Adam to see what he would call them. And whatever Adam called each living creature, that was its name. So Adam gave names to all cattle, to the birds of the air, and every beast of the field. But for Adam, there was not found a helper comparable to him*". (Genesis 2:18–20).

The Word *brought* carries a special meaning and assignment. All that God created was brought to Adam to see what he would call them. Something must happen to man, or man must experience something for him, to say something. The word *brought* in the Hebrew is "*bow*" or "bw" which means: to come to, to gather in, and cohabit with. Adam did not just begin to name everything continuously. Adam became knowledgeable and understood the nature of each living creature to give a name to its being. As Adam cohabited with all things, the purpose and nature of all things were revealed to him and he named them accordingly. Adam witnessed their mating and birthing of young and living among each and observed their purpose. Adam had moments of touching and handling all things that God made. There was no essence of time, so we cannot refer to time, as to how long it took to name everything.

Do you remember after Jesus's resurrection and just before His ascension, His disciples were gathered-together, and He appeared? They were terrified and frightened, and Jesus said, *"Why are you troubled? And why do doubts arise in your hearts? Behold My hands and My feet, that it is I Myself. Handle Me and see, for a spirit does not have flesh and bones as you see I have"* (Luke 24:38- 39). Jesus **brought** Himself to His disciples. For His disciples to completely understand and comprehension His presence and message, they had to handle Him to come to full acceptance to know He is the Christ.

God already said, *"It is not good that man should be alone; I will make him a helper comparable to him"* (Genesis 2:18). Now that Adam have cohabited, handled, named, and understood the nature and purpose of God's creation, he now knows and understands his needs. As we live and continue in obedience to God, He will take responsibility to provide for our needs.

*"Then the rib which the Lord God had taken from man He made into a woman, and He **brought** (bow or bw) her to the man"* (Genesis 2:22).

As we continue to study the word *brought* in the Concise Hebrew Aramaic Lexicon it also means to penetrate, to come upon. Based on the definition, I am sure there was penetration, sexual relationship, when God *"brought"* the woman to the man. It was God who gave the gift of sex and instituted the first sexual experience. I envision the presentation of the woman to Adam supersedes any thought and reasoning of the human mind. It was a presentation by a Holy God, righteous in nature with complete purity in His thought, methodical in His concepts, and completely honest in His intent. In the biblical text, *And the* LORD *God said, "It is not good that man should be alone; I will make him a helper comparable to him"* (Genesis 2:18). The statement, *"a helper comparable"* I am convinced He meant someone comparable to bring sexual fulfillment as well. It is God who gave the sexual desire and ultimately total fulfilment. It was an experience without any inhibitions, ungodly thoughts, any restrictions, and to be fully engaged in God's presence. It is God who gave the sexual desire. It was God who built the human anatomy to be aroused by the opposite sex. I do not believe there are any words in any dictionary or mind of man that can come close in explaining what Adam and Eve experienced. They lived with each other in and with the nature of God. It was the nature of God releasing the expressions of God to each other. As they pleased God, God released the same pleasure of pleasing each other. I believe there was an inexpressible exposure of God to Adam and Eve that carried them into a deeper significance of God's presence with one another that He wants to give to husbands and wives even today.

I believe Satan was exceptionally angry about this relationship Adam and Eve was experiencing with each other and they with God. He understood praise and worship but not at this dimension. Satan praised God and worshipped God's person and existence, but He could not experience the joy of giving to another this entity of creation. It was a joy he had never known and could not ever experience himself. He could only witness it. Can you imagine the envy and anger of Satan? From then and until now, Satan's aim is to completely extirpate everything God gave to Adam and Eve and mankind. Now, do not forget, this was not just a one-time experience Adam and Eve enjoyed. During this period of human living, there was no such thing as time. It was eons and eons upon eons, no measure of anything such as time. There isn't any aging, constant energy, and without tiring. Can you possibly imagine living with a concept of nothing ending? If Adam and Eve were here to testify of the awesomeness and unexplainable pleasure experienced by the married couple, I believe their testimony would be, "and we still can't explain or tell it all".

And we know that anything and everything God made and gave was good. When completed with creation, He called all of creation, "*very good*". By Him saying "*very good*" it is acceptable to say that everything about the man is "*very good*". It was after the sexual experience (handling and exploring all of Eve and Eve handling and exploring all of Adam) that Adam now understood the nature of the woman and their relationship to one another and the purpose of their being. The first Word of Knowledge came as Adam spoke of the relationship between man and woman.

> And Adam said: *"This is now bone of my bones And flesh of my flesh; She shall be called Woman, Because she was taken out of Man." Therefore a man shall leave his father and mother and be joined to his wife, and they shall become one flesh"* (Genesis 2:23–24).

This is now the self, the substance of myself, and the singular divine construction of me, and this pattern will continue as fathers and mothers produce divine structures, leaving father and mother. The man will continue to become one flesh with the woman, the wife.

CHAPTER THREE

IT IS MINISTRY

"Everything that we do—eating, sleeping, talking with our friends, conducting business, even sexual intercourse—everything should be done in a way that will glorify the Lord".

—Lester Sumrall

"Therefore, whether you eat or drink, or whatever you do, do all to the glory of God"
— (1 Corinthians 10:31)

There is nothing X-Rated between the Christian husband and wife's sexual activities and discussions.

MINISTERING IS TO give all of oneself to God for another. In the beginning, with Adam and Eve, they had eons of time to give to each other all that God gave to them for each other. I am convinced that God intended for sex to be weaved and structured in man's relationship to God. It begins with loving God with all of your soul, mind, and body to give all of oneself to God while God pours all of Himself to others through you.

> ". . . . . *You shall love the* LORD *your God with all your heart, with all your soul, and with all your mind".* (Matthew 22:37)

As we open the Bible text, I pray that you will also open your mind and spirit to see that God gave to mankind sex and the sex drive. Even though God gave to man a sex drive, it is also expected to be identified and used for the intent God gave. When God made man, His expression about the man He made was, "*very good*". When God makes anything, it is wrong to say of anything within or about what He made is bad or evil.

When God gave sex to man it was intended to be included as a form of worship given back to Him as well as for Adam and Eve to fully minister to each other while propagating the human race. And Adam said, "*This is now bone of my bone and flesh of my flesh; She shall be called Woman, Because she was taken out of Man*" (Genesis 2:23). Adam did not just look at Eve, he handled her, he explored her, as he fully experienced her. The harmony and oneness that Adam and Eve lived before the fall were beyond any human's ability to fully explain. They experienced a gift from God without total comprehension but with a praise of thanksgiving. In our lives today, we give God thanks for everything— our salvation, our health, our family, our employment, — everything but our sexual experience of husband and wife. It is because we have not been taught that we should.

In the absence of praise and worship to God, we are left with the psychological makeup of a man's mind open to his own thoughts and delusions which could leave him without the concepts of the original intent of God. *"I will bless the Lord at all times; His praise shall continually be in my mouth"* (Psalm 34:1). Before the fall in Genesis 3, everything Adam and Eve did was a praise to God and a worship to His being. *"According to Your name, O God, So is Your praise to the ends of the earth; Your right hand is full of righteousness"* (Psalm 48:10).

You may say, there aren't any instructions to Adam and Eve to praise and worship God. Even though it was not stated to Adam and Eve, it was built in their DNA, *"Let Us make man in Our image, according to Our likeness;"* (Genesis 1:26). It is written in Eph 5:20, *"giving thanks always for all things to God the Father in the name of our Lord Jesus Christ,"* which carries the expected expression of all mankind.

> *"But You are holy, Enthroned in the praises of Israel"*
> (Psalm 22:3).

In the sacrificial death and victorious resurrection of Jesus Christ, He bought back to mankind what was lost in the fall of Genesis 3. The sacrificial death and victorious resurrection of Jesus not only paid the price for redemption but also restored to man the life Adam and Eve lived with each other before the fall. They lived experiencing the precious presence of God's glory without time. And for the lack of any other words to use, they had moments without any consciousness of anything natural or human activity. Moments of transcendent purity of thought. Every expression untainted with guilt or shame, accompanied with all activities of pure reverence. Those moments, where human language has no components of description. All that could be said is GLORY! That is how Adam and Eve lived for eons. Everything Adam and Eve did was divinely sanctioned by God and a worship unto God our Creator. Worship is a Hebrew word: *shachah* – meaning, prostrate, in homage to royalty or God. It is to cast oneself face down, reduced to helplessness. It is simply to dethrone self.

Before the fall, everything Adam and Eve did glorified God. That included their sexual experiences as well. It was as much as worship as lifting the hands. As they lifted their hands in praise to God, they ministered to God from the inward dwelling of God's image and likeness. How can their sexual encounters be excluded? As they danced before Him, how can their sexual encounters be excluded? As they open their mouths to give God a shout and praise, how can their sexual encounters be excluded? As they sexually came together, their minds were not contaminated with shame, perversion, and immoral thoughts. All and everything they did was Holy and a reverence to God.

SATAN'S INTERFERENCE

Genesis 2:25 reads, *"And they were both naked, the man and his wife, and were not ashamed,"* is the proof of their total innocence of any shame with each other and was totally accepted by God. Naked is how God presented Eve to Adam.

Along with Satan deceiving Eve and Adam being tempted, I say again, I believe Satan also wanted to destroy the awesome ministering that Adam and Eve shared with each other. I also believe Satan knew what he was doing, attempting to ultimately destroy the sanctity of this precious gift that God gave to mankind to be included in worship to God. Stay with me as we unfold the text.

Genesis 2:16-17, reads, *"And the Lord God commanded the man, saying, "Of every tree of the garden you may freely eat; but of the tree of the knowledge of good and evil you shall not eat, for in the day that you eat of it you shall surely die."* The reference for living or dying was eating or not eating the forbidden fruit. I understand that scriptural text leaves us to believe Satan had just this one conversation with Eve. I believe he had several. Eve was too comfortable in her dialogue with Satan. He tapped into her emotions by putting a question in her mind about what Adam had taught her and a living desire to do something independent of her husband. Her independent desire to do something her husband didn't say relieved her mind to be open to deception.

To the wives, never allow anyone, other than your God given husband minister to you concerning life changing thoughts. Listen to how Satan lured her into conversing with him.

> *"Now the serpent was more cunning than any beast of the field which the LORD God had made. And he said to the woman, "Has God indeed said, 'You shall not eat of every tree of the garden'?"* (Genesis 3:1)

Listen to Satan's devious dialogue, 'Eve think for yourself—there is something Adam and God is not telling you'. The wisdom that every wife must utilize is to stand on the truth her husband shared with her and let God be responsible for withheld information.

Eve should have responded, "No, Adam said to me, Of

every tree of the garden we may freely eat, but of the Tree of the Knowledge of Good and Evil, we shall not eat, for in the day that we eat of it, we shall surely die."

It would have silenced Satan because Adam was God's representative, the kingdom of God's ambassador. But because of Eve's independent desire, which Adam never ministered to her, she opened her heart for deception. She even added to the statement, *'nor shall you touch it'*. We are instructed to never add nor take from the Word.

> *"You shall not add to the word which I command you, nor take from it, that you may keep the commandments of the LORD your God which I command you"* (Deuteronomy 4:2).

When you add your thoughts and desires to the Word of God, deception will creep right in and so often you will not detect your deception until your presentation is robbed of honesty and yet filled with guilt.

After the fall in Genesis 3, the referencing of themselves changed from being covered to not being covered. When they heard God coming into the Garden to visit with them, they hid themselves. God called to Adam, *"Where are you?* Adam said, *"I heard Your voice in the garden, and I was afraid because I was naked; and I hid myself"*. - And God said, *"Who told you that you were naked? Have you eaten from the tree of which I commanded you that you should not eat?"* I then ask the Holy Spirit, what does, eating of the fruit have to do with being naked? The Holy Spirit enlightened me that they had been covered with the **glory** of God and all that they were and did was innocent with God and themselves. To be covered by God's glory qualifies all that is done under the glory glorifies God. In the mind of God, Genesis 3:21 existed before the fall of Adam and Eve. *"Also for Adam and his wife the Lord God made tunics of skin and clothed them"*. It was the first blood sacrifice providing a covering for Adam and Eve again. You must remember, Satan never wins, he can only interfere and when he interferes God helps us to make adjustments that are needful and will bless us at the same time. Being covered by the blood provided by God, they were restored back to a state of glory.

> *"Therefore, whether you eat or drink, or whatever you do, do all to the glory of God".* (1 Corinthians 10:31)

I emphasize *"whatever you do"* for there is nothing given to man, other than Jesus Christ, greater than the sexual relationship between man and women (husband & wife). Before the fall of man, everything that man and woman did was praise and worship to God. The sexual encounter was the ultimate expression of God's love in man being expressed to woman and the expression of God's love in woman being expressed to the man. Husbands, as you and your wife minister to each other, it is needful to minister the Word of God as well.

Even after the fall, God has a redemptive plan to restore all that He structured for man. One of Satan's manipulative plans was to cause pleasure to supersede ministering the Word of God while ministering sexual fulfillment to each other. When pleasure become the ultimate of the sexual encounter, praise and worship will vacate and the expressions of love suffers.

TRUTH WILL SET US FREE

Even though we are living after the fall we must never let the blunder of the fall continue to castigate our mind of the fall. God has made it possible for the husband and wife to continue experiencing all that was given before the fall. We have more to shout about as we celebrate victories over the Devil. While we shout and praise God for many types of blessings: healing of the body, cured of a life-threatening disease, a new home, a new car, a substantial raise on your job, we must include the precious gift of sex given to the husband and wife. There is no greater way for the husband to express godly and genuine love to his wife and there is no greater way for the wife to express godly and genuine love to her husband than an open and unashamed fulfilling sexual encounter. Now that we understand that it was instituted by God and is a gift from God, we should, without any reservations, praise God for it and to worship Him as husband and wife minister to each other with an attitude of thankfulness toward God. If you, husband, or wife, ever begin to notice less expressions of love and a laboring to purpose fulfillment, quickly repent and restore to the marriage an atmosphere of worship and gratitude to God with loving expression to each other.

FULL AND COMPLETE ATTENTION IS AN EXPRESSION OF LOVE AND APPRECIATION

I asked several women, "In a sexual encounter with your husband, what is your greatest need or want, sexual satisfaction or his full attention?" Several said, "sexual satisfaction", but the majority said, "his full attention". When a man gives his wife "full attention" it is an expression of him wanting to please and bring satisfaction to his wife in every aspect. Full attention is an expression of his love, appreciation, and intentions to satisfy completely and wholly. She will not only experience his full presence and attention but will also sense the presence of God in the relationship. When a woman lives with her husband and she is not only told but shown that she is first (other than God) in his life, she lives to bring him ultimate satisfaction and praise to God for him. Adam and Eve lived a life, before the fall, fully and always filled with God's presence and fully engaged with one another. There was absolutely no shame in all things.

CHAPTER FOUR

INTENDED FOR PLEASURE

G OD INTENDED FOR the pleasure of sex to continue in building a stronger relationship between husband and wife and a reverence and thankfulness to God. Yet, if sex is only for pleasure you have already missed the point of this entire book. Many couples, even Christian couples, have engaged in sex before marriage and have made a life commitment based on the pleasure each has experienced. This kind of marriage will not have the element of continual new experiences each time of engagement. Their love, if there was any, becomes stagnated and sex could become a chore and boring, especially for the wife.

To be born again by the Spirit of God is first and foremost the greatest gift that God has given to man who believes in the blood and resurrection of Jesus Christ. The second is the filling of the Holy Spirit. The next gift that is given to man is marital sex and the highest expression of love between husband and wife.

"Marriage is honorable among all, and the bed undefiled; . . . . . ." Hebrews 13:4

From Genesis to Revelations, God never said anything negative or given any type of inhibitions to sex in a marriage. He only spoke of the negative aspects of the disorder and misplacement of the purpose and intent: fornication, (sex before marriage): adultery, (a married person having sex with another married or single person): or prostitution, (sex with others for positional achievement or money). Satan is a thief, and he comes only to steal, kill, and destroy. A thief does not strive to steal anything that is of no value to you or the Kingdom of God.

SEX WAS PURPOSED ONLY FOR THE MARITAL BOND

When the order of God is respected, His reason for the order is revealed. In the animal kingdom, you will never see babies having babies. The principle is clear, the young are not brought forth until they can be properly cared for. In the order of God there is first the man, the home, provisions for living, the wife, the mother, then children. If sex had remained only in the marital bond, we would never have the problems we have in our society today. The problems with sexual transmitted diseases, children without fathers, unwanted pregnancies, which has engendered the need for foster care and orphanages. Then the over-populated foster homes and orphanages created another problem known as abortion - which is simply murder. I always say, "If Satan strives to use and prosper from anything, it must be of value and spiritual significant for the believer when used in God's order". Yes, God intended for sex to be pleasurable. But when pleasure is the only view and thought of sex, the respect for God's order is grossly violated. When in God's ordained order, it is God Himself who builds a level of pleasure that will leave an indelible impression on the minds of both husband and wife. When pleasure is fortified with Godly love, it will continue to build a union that can stand in difficult times.

When there is an understanding of God's purpose and His position on the sexual relationship of husband and wife, it creates an alacrity in both. Remember, it was God who gave the gift of sex and instituted the first sexual experience. And we know that everything God gave was good. When completed with creation, He called all of creation, *"very good"*. By Him saying, *"very good"*, it is acceptable to say that everything about the man and for man is *"very good"*. It was intended, as a means, to keep the reverence, devotion, and commitment to godly and holy living in the human race beginning with the first husband and wife. The migration of that truth was to continue through all generations.

When the knowledge of good and evil was discovered by man, a potential of evil evolved within the nature of man concerning sex. The spirit of that evil was released into an atmosphere of evil potential. Sex itself is an extremely, unmeasurable precious gift given to the husband and wife. Satan's aim behind his persuasion for the forbidden fruit to be eaten was not only to create a separation of man and God, but also to birth a potential evil in man to abuse the precious and perfect gift of sex. That is why Adam said to God, *"I heard Your voice in the garden, and I was afraid because I was naked; and I hid myself"* (Genesis 3:10). They were robbed of their natural innocence to appreciation, the touching, handling, pleasing, and being pleased with the bodies God gave to each of them. Satan saw the awesome, pleasurable, peaceful, enjoyable, and Godly expressions that both Adam and Eve experienced in their sexual encounter. He knew that it would suffer after the fall as well.

I asked God, why didn't I see this before? He responded, "All things that are valuable and precious, are kept in a special environment, the diamond, the pearl, and the ruby are revealed at it's given time". It is a truth that revelation is only released when information can be properly ascertained and assimilated.

GOD HAS GIVEN YOU THE ENERGY TO GIVE

Listen, God gave the sex drive and the pleasure of sex. The husband and the wife should do to the best of their knowledge and communal agreement to please each other with the same expression that God had when He made man.

> *"Then God saw everything that He had made, and indeed it was very good"* (Genesis 1:31).

I believe, when God said, *"It's not good for man to be alone"* it was also inclusive of fulfilling the sexual desires He gave to husband and wife, as well as their cooperative working together. Because of the love you have for each other, the energy of love should be the driving force to do all that you know and are capable of, to bring the maximum fulfillment to your mate. The more you thank God and praise Him for the gift of sex to the marriage, the richer each encounter can be. When all things are kept in proper perspective and order, there is no limit to the joy, pleasure, and love that the married couple can experience. Remember, God Himself is limitless. Being that there is no end to anything in God, when everything that He is, is respected and praised can become greater in its expressions and understanding. God is the only one who can add to the epitome of an encounter. As we read His word, our knowledge of God will increase. As we receive His word, faith and revelation should increase. As we pray, wisdom and relationship should increase. Keeping God amid all we do leaves all our encounters in life limitless in their experiences. In the God-ordained and purposed marriage, the glory of God is present in each sexual encounter. Since there is no limit in God and we can never experience all of who God is, is why the pleasure of each sexual encounter seems to be greater than the previous. As we worship and praise Him in all that we do, there is a richness and joy that we experience that will always seem greater than yesterday.

SEX SHOULD BE OFTEN

There are too many Christians who have been tainted by misconceptions, incorrect information, and wrong teachings about sex, have the understanding that it is an interruption to bible study and their prayer life.

I was teaching in a marriage seminar once and a female minister came to me during a break and she stated that her husband was always complaining about the lack of sex in their marriage. I asked why? She replied, "I believe that sex hinders the anointing on my life". I said, "you have deceived yourself or you have been deceived". I asked her, "how often are you and you husband having sex"? She said, "maybe once a month, and whenever I'm not ministering". I inquired, "what is your husband saying about this and how is he handling it"? She said, "he has to understand". My last word to her was, "you are ministering everywhere else and leaving your first responsibility of ministry at home. Mam, I promise you, go home, initiate a sexual encounter with your husband each week and watch your marriage blossom and your revelation and freedom in ministering increase". Well, she did not fully agree, but she took my advice. Approximately six months passed, I received a phone call from her and her husband, thanking me for the advice. In her reply, she said, "I sense my husband's love on a deeper level and my freedom as I minister is unbelievable". It is true that everything in life must have balance and proper assessment of activities, but you cannot violate scripture and call it spiritual.

> *"Do not deprive one another except with consent for a time, that you may give yourselves to fasting and prayer; and come together again so that Satan does not tempt you because of your lack of self-control"* (1 Corinthians 7:5).

When the sex life suffers, other unforeseen problems will birth and escalate, and you will not realize they evolved from your sexual neglect. Godly and pleasurable sex will always leave an impression on the mind and will clear up any unsolved differences in your relationship. As the husband and wife build a healthy, godly sex life, they will consciously and purposely fight and give everything that is in them to destroy any seed of disunity and disruption that would come against or between them. Christian couples who are experiencing biblically structured sexual experiences are having countless days of joy and happiness. And like others who have not purposed to do so, are having fewer days of joy and happiness, along with more days of sadness and pain.

I asked several men who strongly confess their Christian faith, "What would they rather have: a million dollars, or sex with their wives daily?" Their answers were unanimous, "Sex with their wives on a daily basis". When wives understand that it is normal for her husband to want sex daily, she will be relieved of the ungodly accusations that Satan offers to her thinking. When the husband and wife are doing the maximum to bring total pleasure to the other. It is a love that can never be expressed in any other form. As a matter of fact, it is a love embedded within the Spirit of God living in the husband and wife. Within the nature and being of God, there is no limit to the expressions of His love. The Spirit of God still calls everything that God made, "very good".

The only time sex is to be withheld from your mate, is when it is an agreed-upon time of fasting and praying. The Bible emphasizes, "as soon as the fast is over, come back together ASAP".

> *"Do not deprive one another except with consent for a time, that you may give yourselves to fasting and prayer; and come together again so that Satan does not tempt you because of your lack of self-control"* (1 Corinthians 7:5).

To deprive your mate of sex should never be used as a tool to punish or manipulate. To deny your mate for any other reason than fasting or physical challenges, you are not only building a wall of disunity, you are also disobeying God. It should be a serious effort, first in your spirit and mind, to minister to your mate for the maximum of pleasure. It is an expression of love. When the angel came to Abraham in Genesis 18 and said that he and Sarah would have a child, Sarah was in the tent and laughed, saying, "After I have grown old, shall I have the pleasure (sexual delight) with my lord being old also?" As we notice in Genesis 16, it was a child that Sarah expressed she so desperately wanted, not pleasure. But when the Angel told Abraham that she would have a child, she expressed what she had experienced with Abraham. She did not have the pleasure of a child but the remembrance of the pleasure of sex was richly living in her mind.

> *"Let the husband render to his wife the affection due her, and likewise also the wife to her husband"* (1 Corinthians 7:3).

The word "due" is a word that should never be taken lightly. When you are serious about fulfilling the sexual desires and needs of your mate, it is a statement of love that can never be expressed in any other capacity. When sexual pleasure and praise are combined in their expressions, it robs the Devil of any guilt that He tries to induce into the mind of the wife or the husband. You should NEVER feel guilty of having great, refreshing, explosive, boundless, and pleasurable sex.

> *The husband should fulfill his wife's sexual needs, and the wife should fulfill her husband's needs. The wife gives authority over her body to her husband, and the husband gives authority over his body to his wife.*

Do not deprive each other of sexual relations unless you both agree to refrain from sexual intimacy for a limited time so you can give yourselves more completely to prayer. Afterward, you should come together again so that Satan will not be able to tempt you because of your lack of self-control" (1 Corinthians 7:3–5, NLT).

CHAPTER FIVE

THE LANGUAGE OF SEX

N ow that you know that God gave to the marriage sexual cohesiveness, joy, and fulfillment, many couples live with the missing dimension of open communication. It is amazing how freely and uninhibited the home of married couples are when it comes to discussing the home budget, activities of savings and retirement, children's education, home buying, buying furniture, and so forth. But when it comes to the closest most valuable time of relating to each other as husband and wife, there is still a serious deficiency. I have found, in many years of counseling, the average couple still lives with a problem of openly discussing personal preferences, desires, and wants in sexual intimacy. I must remind you that God gave to the man and woman sexual pleasure with its desires, feelings, emotions, and satisfying gratification. When there is a problem to freely communicate desires, mythologies, and preference, so often one of the two, or both, leaves the moment with unfulfilled wishes and desires.

So many, mostly wives, feel cheated and sometimes even used.

It is often said the husband is the hindrance of an unpleasant sexual encounter. If you, wife, do not stop and take a moment to explain your desires, wants, and needs, you are just as guilty. Before your love for one another begins to suffer and become attacked, stop and lovingly say to your mate with as much love and tenderness, without being ashamed, the things you are missing as well as a method to accommodate your needs or desires of fulfillment. Wives, just as you discuss with your beautician how you want your hair, in detail, you should be just that open with your husband about your desires before, during, and after you and your husband's intimate encounters.

Husbands, just as you tell your wife how you prefer your eggs or favorite dish, you should be that open and clear about your sexual preference and desires. Take the time to explain your desires, which will slow down your moment of release. It is wise to talk about what you would love to do to and for each other. The more detailed you are in your expressions and methodologies, the closer your trust and freedom in your relationship will become.

> "Marriage is honorable among all, and the bed undefiled; . . . ." (Hebrews 13:4).

Words are powerful when expressed from a heart of love. The right words will come easily when the attitude of pleasing your mate is as strong as the need for your fulfillment and sexual satisfaction. Set designated times, as husband and wife, to openly say and show each other the things that will bring you pleasure. Words will slow down the rate of reaching full gratification when they are used to express and explain your actions while doing what pleases your mate.

In my experience of counseling others, some affairs were triggered when another man or woman has freely expressed a thought or subject, without reservations, while the husband or wife are having inhibitions in discussing what they wanted to hear from their mate. Sexual language is a fellowship and ministering of husband and wife is especially important. It tells the other mate that you trust them with something that is very dear to you. It is also said, without saying, how much your mate trusts you and you trusting your mate with something that is so deeply personal. Your love for your mate should encourage you to destroy any language barriers hindering any expressions that are the deepest of your personal self to one another.

When there is a freedom to share openly with each other your desires, actions, wants, methodologies, and diplomacies, the experiences will develop a deeper sense of love and trust. When the language is inhibited, so often sexual encounters are filled with assumptions that expectations are fulfilled. Assumptions can ruin your sex life because your mate just might have unspoken moments of unfulfillment, and disappointment will begin to live in the heart. Disappointment will rob desire and hinder pleasurable satisfaction. TALK! you talk about everything else, TALK! like you talk about other matters in life.

God made your body with those desires. When there are no assumptions and yet an explicit open dialogue while engaged in your sexual encounters, your heart will be open to experience another unlimited level of love that the Spirit of God will embrace. Even as you as a couple have your private discussions during phone conversations, let your heart be free. Remember, the other person is your mate, your love, and your heart, and you are one.

DO NOT LET LIFE'S DEMANDS RUIN INTIMACY

In a marriage where the husband's or wife's schedule, or both, is extremely full and chaotic, stop trusting signs, or gesticulations, for sexual attention in hopes for sexual fulfillment. It is possible that none may register in the mind of your mate. The pressures of life and living can so often become very strenuous and over challenging. It is not that they did not notice, it is their conscious level that has been preoccupied with more details, actions, or planning than the norm. The human mind has limitations to properly analyze several thoughts at a 100 percent level. The last fully engaged thought is most often the present engagement of thinking. So, what is presently seen does not get immediate attention.

True, for your mate to seemingly ignore your loving gestures is cruel and unfair and could be painful. Yes, you may be thinking that you have made them so obvious and extremely detectable, yet you have been ignored. Remember, so far, only one person is speaking. You cannot come to a balanced understanding with a one-sided conversation. Touching, smiling, and loving words, all done together, are the best language that you can speak during these moments until both minds are galvanized on identical subjects. The virtue of patience must be employed during these times. You must exercise, love, patience, and wisdom. Your word preferences must be suitable to cause the mind to willingly dismiss the present occupancies and welcome a new thought to become resident in the mind. Choose words that will address the present state and condition to be an acceptable replacement of words previously used. Example: "Honey, why are so grumpy and impatient?" to be replaced with, "Honey, with gentle touching, you seem a little tense, what can I do to help you relax?" For most men, that is all it will take. But with the woman, men listen, so often you are only beginning to dissolve the pre-existing trains of thoughts. If there are children, and the wife works outside the home, her first thoughts are of the children and then dinner for her family. Sex is not the initial thought on her mind. She could be thinking of it, but it does not register as NOW. If all are home and the children are yet young and not teenagers, man/husband, put on something that your wife admires for you to wear and assist her with the children, or dinner, or anything to help relieve her of any evening details or duties. Do it without asking. As you are helping and completing the evening details, quietly express to her, without invitations, and without any demands, things you would love to do for her and to her for her pleasure and relaxation. Give her soft-unexpected touches mixed with words of appreciation. Her mind must be relaxed before her body can respond.

Because so many couples are daily strained with details and responsibilities, total exhaustion inhibits a pleasurable time to engage with your mate. When total exhaustion robs you of that moment, verbal communication becomes a problem. Speaking with a note pad of an apology and expressions of love and appreciation can so often ease the moment of frustration and disappointment rather than the expression of your emotions, mixed with anger and hurt. Never tell your mate things like, "You never show me any attention". Guilt may cause a sexual encounter, but it may birth a wave of unexpressed anger. Just to experience a sexual release or relief may not be embraced with love, and often-times some displeasure is experienced. For that moment, the Spirit of God will not be engaged. Many arguments are birthed before or after such encounters. A silent anger could be developing like a freight train, coming down the track, if you do not take a moment to pull the splinter out of the heart.

LET GOD BE PLEASED WITH YOUR WORDS

As you understand that it is pleasing to God to love your husband and the husband to love his wife with the intent to totally please, not only sexually, godly love is expressed through you to your mate. When this is not done, due to ignorance, pride, or selfishness, a deeper level of enjoyment and fulfillment will never be experienced.

I want you to think of that moment when you refused a thought of thankfulness to God or praise to Him during that special moment, because you thought it to be inappropriate or uncomfortable. I tell you that, God prompted it and He was waiting for the praise. The more you learn and is revealed to you of God's approval of the husband and wife's intimate uninhibited moments, the more open your expressions will become, and your vocabulary will increase.

CHAPTER SIX

BODY LANGUAGE

Y OUR WORDS SHOULD speak loud and descriptive while your body is complementing what you have spoken. Can we just stop for a moment to simply see the truth of the Word of God? "And the Lord God **formed** man of the dust of the ground" (Genesis 2:7). "Then the rib which the Lord God had taken from man He made into a woman" (Genesis 2:22).

If I know anything about God, He does not do anything less than "*very good*, the best, the greatest, wonderful, marvelous, and grand". I believe He has given me the liberty to say, "WOW!" To admire the body of the man and woman without giving thanks to the creator of such beauty could open the door to the perversion that is spreading through our world today. Husband and wife, it is godly and expected of God our Creator, to express your heart of how appreciative you are of your mate's (God's created frame) body as you give thanks to Him for the framework that excites you. It does not matter the state and condition of the body's development. It is the display and verbal expressions, as well as the action of doing things to address the body, you want to present to your mate. Husbands, if you are pressing your wife to stay fit and pleasing to you, you should place that same expectations on yourself. Your willingness to work on your own body will give your wife a greater determination to do the same without the constant pressure on her for fitness. **Both husband and wife should honor God in maintaining the pulchritude that He made and gave when He formed you.** Take moments to express praise and thankfulness to God for your body and your mate's body. The Spirit of God will impact your will to keep yourself pleasing, first to God, next to your mate, and lastly to yourself.

<u>Treat God's temple with respect and He</u>
<u>will be present to help you.</u>

The Spirit of God moved on Solomon to pen a book speaking of these principles for all of mankind. "Your breasts are like fawns, twins of a gazelle, grazing among the first spring flowers" (Song of Solomon 4:5, MSG).

"You've captured my heart, dear friend. You looked at me, and I fell in love. One look my way and I was hopelessly in love!" (Song of Solomon 4:9, MSG).

"The kisses of your lips are honey, my love, every syllable you speak a delicacy to savor. Your clothes smell like the wild outdoors, the ozone scent of high mountains" (Song of Solomon 4:11, MSG).

The heart of God desires for you to verbally praise your mate's body. Your verbal praise glorifies God for the body He made

Himself. It is pleasing to God and your mate to openly admire each other, yes, the body He gave to you.

> *"Shapely and graceful your sandaled feet, and queenly your movement— Your limbs are lithe and elegant, the work of a master artist. Your body is a chalice, wine-filled. Your skin is silken and tawny like a field of wheat touched by the breeze. Your breasts are like fawns, twins of a gazelle. Your neck is carved ivory, curved and slender. Your eyes are wells of light, deep with mystery. Quintessentially feminine! Your profile turns all heads, commanding attention. The feelings I get when I see the high mountain ranges —stirrings of desire, longings for the heights— Remind me of you, and I am spoiled for anyone else! Your beauty, within and without, is absolute, dear lover, close companion. You are tall and supple, like the palm tree, and your full breasts are like sweet clusters of dates. I say, "I'm going to climb that palm tree! I'm going to caress its fruit!" Oh yes! Your breasts will be clusters of sweet fruit to me, Your breath clean and cool like fresh mint, your tongue and lips like the best wine. Yes, and yours are, too—my love's kisses flow from his lips to mind"* (Song of Solomon 7:1–9, MSG).

In Song of Solomon, there are many words that speak of the body of the woman and man. It is also evident that the reference identifies a maintained body. Maintaining the body is an honor to God as you care for the body He made.

How beautiful are your feet in sandals, O prince's daughter! The curves of your thighs are like jewels, The work of the hands of a skillful workman. Your navel is a rounded goblet; It lacks no blended beverage. Your waist is a heap of wheat Set about with lilies. Your two breasts are like two fawns, Twins of a gazelle. Your neck is like an ivory tower, Your eyes like the pools in Heshbon, by the gate of Bath Rabbim. Your nose is like the tower of Lebanon Which looks toward Damascus (Song of Solomon 7:1–4).

His head is like the finest gold; His locks are wavy, And black as a raven. His eyes are like doves by the rivers of waters, washed with milk, and fitly set. His cheeks are like a bed of spices, Banks of scented herbs. His lips are lilies, Dripping liquid myrrh. His hands are rods of gold Set with beryl. His body is carved ivory Inlaid with sapphires. His legs are pillars of marble Set on bases of fine gold. His countenance is like Lebanon, Excellent as the cedars. His mouth is most sweet, Yes, he is altogether lovely. This is my beloved, And this is my friend, O daughters of Jerusalem! (Song of Solomon 5:11–16).

By the descriptions in some of the text, it is obvious that the passages depict their bodies to be fully unclothed, fit, and maintained. When you properly care for your body, it is a language to your mate that you care enough to present a gift of love and appreciation. It is an expression to say, "I love you to the point that I want you to always be pleased with what you see". And just as important, your body is God's temple, and He is pleased also that you honor the body that He made and presented to you and your mate. When your mate sees that you are always concerned about presentation and observation, it is an unspoken statement of, "I love you so much". The words spoken by presentation carries just as much (sometimes more) weight as daily words of, "I love you".

To display neglect of caring for the body will slowly hinder genuine intimacy. Your mate could see it as an unspoken statement of diminishing love. Unattended bodies (male and female) can hinder moments of spontaneous encounters. Spontaneous encounters are mainly prompted by physical attraction associated by words of appreciation.

> *Or do you not know that your body is the temple of the Holy Spirit who is in you, whom you have from God, and you are not your own? For you were bought at a price; therefore, **glorify God** in your body and in your spirit, which are God's* (1 Corinthians 6:19–20).

The scripture is not only speaking of your life behavior and conduct but as well as the upkeep of His body. Think about it: what condition is the house that God lives in? Would you put your father or mother in a run-down, unfit, unpainted house with bulging walls? Why would we present to God a house that He lives in to be that way? When we keep our body free of sin and clean, it glorifies God. Well, when we keep our body fit and conditioned it glorifies God as well. It is also a Godly presentation of His goodness and your discipline. Notice, I did not say skinny and trimmed but fit and conditioned. You should have an attitude and concern of presentation just as much as appreciation. The right presentation will always be granted with the appropriate appreciation which will enhance an already loving attraction. You should always be concerned about your mate's attraction to you and God's appreciation of you. The proper presentation will provoke words of appreciation and glorification which will inevitably invigorate a moment of gratification. **"Do you hear me?"**

MEN ARE VISUAL AND WOMEN ARE PHYSICAL

So many women have criticized men for their attraction and appreciation of the female body. I cannot and will not justify the perverted aspect of some men. Let us just speak of your husband or the man engaged to you. If there is any type of perversion or ungodly thoughts in him, you have a responsibility to pray for him. The God in him will convict him of any type of perversion. God did many things that we will never be able to know why and cannot understand.

> *"Know ye that the LORD he is God: it is He who that hath made us, and not we ourselves; . . . .* (Psalms 100:3).

I do not believe that men being visual is any fault of man himself. God made him that way. In the book of Genesis, Jacob expressed his visual aspect when he saw and kissed Rachel. The Bible says that Jacob cried out loud because of the beauty of Rachel. My translation of the text would be, "He screamed when he saw

Rachel". The text of Genesis 29:17 says, *"Rachel was beautiful of form and appearance"*. The NET translation says, *"but Rachel had a lovely figure and beautiful appearance"*. Rachel's <u>person</u> and <u>her body</u> spoke a language that caused Jacob to labor an additional seven years for her.

Ladies, so often, you can say more lasting and motivating words of love with your body than words from your mouth. What he sees will birth thoughts, words, and actions that will generate a smile in his heart that will manifest a smile on your face. When a woman is pleasing to the sight of her husband, it will make it easy for him to fulfill her unspoken physical expectations. He will say to his wife glorious and sexual statements about her and her person while touching and caressing her body all at the same time. Since he is visual, use it to your advantage by keeping yourself on his mind during the course of his day. During his day, he will have repeated thoughts to pop-up in his mind of his wife and not the perverted temptation of thoughts.

> *"and I'm spoiled for anyone else!"* (Song of Solomon 7:5 MSG).

Brethren, when you take time to tone-up your body, it is an invitation to the wife to touch and massage with tenderness and appreciation. Having a want to maintain a healthy and attractive body for you and your mate speaks volumes of love and Godly fellowship. When God is your first thought of fitness, conditioning, and maintaining His body, He gives an unspoken abundance of grace and peace to a husband and wife.

"If anyone defiles the temple of God, God will destroy him. For the temple of God is holy, which temple you are" (1 Corinthians 3:17).

An additional component of motivation is the originally intended moments of Genesis 2:25, moments of unplanned sexual gratification.

"And they were both naked, the man and his wife, and were not ashamed" (Genesis 2:25).

When God redeemed us through the blood of Jesus Christ, He brought back to us and for us what Adam and Eve lost. *Re –* means: go back to the original. Husbands and wives, you should put a demand on yourselves to have moments of unashamed, unclothed dwelling together, that is moments of unashamed dwelling while doing things of normality, for instance, watching a movie, cleaning your home, even preparing and having breakfast together and so forth. To have absolutely no shame is a holy platform of expressions of love and trust that can NEVER be expressed verbally. Especially for the woman, when she knows that her husband is pleased with her inward person and is complimented by her physical presentation, she is confident of longevity. Ask yourself, why did God put Genesis 2:25 in the Word of God?

"And they were both naked, the man and his wife, and were not ashamed".

I believe that He intended for the husband and wife to

experience a level of love and trust beyond human expressions while promoting a oneness that would be extremely difficult to destroy. It would generate a lasting desire and determination to maintain the body, fit for presentation. It is fulfilling for women when they hear words of appreciation of their physical anatomy associated with touches of admiration. Brethren, as she works hard to maintain her godly figure, never deprive her of hearing words of appreciation and admiration. You should make special efforts to express words of admiration, as she sets forth efforts to develop and maintain her body. You are expressing, "I love you" in a form that leaves lasting impressions.

Brethren, you should never express or push your mate to maintain a bodily figure that pleases you when your abdomen has greater dimensions than your rump or you cannot see your shoes without bending over. A determination to maintain your body will give her unspoken encouragement to do the same. If the drive and expectations are for her only, you are building in her heart resentment toward your one-sided and selfish expectations.

> "So husbands ought to love their own wives as their own bodies; he who loves his wife loves himself. For no one ever hated his own flesh, but nourishes and cherishes it, just as the Lord does the church" (Ephesians 5:28–29).

Husband, the presentation of your maintained body, without words of criticism, will promote conversations to discuss methods of unified activities while setting goals for fitness. The virtue of unity accomplishing an unspoken desire is glorious.

"According as his divine power hath given unto us all things that pertain unto life and godliness, through the knowledge of him that hath called __us__ to glory and virtue". (2 Peter 1:3, KJV)

When your presentation is not motivated by a love for God and your mate, it affirms little appreciation and love for yourself. When a husband or wife understands the power of presentation of an internal inspiration, God is glorified and He, Himself, will manifest an appreciation and a loving proclamation birthing a heavenly gratification.

CHAPTER SEVEN

THE DIFFICULT TIMES

As LONG AS we are living in mortal flesh, we will have times when there will be a need for readjustments, realignments, rededication, repentance, and forgiveness. That we know this, it is wisdom to prepare for these difficult times by discussing each stage with each other. It is wisdom to consciously avoid any negative thinking, statements, and negative confessions. Growing older and getting older is a fact. Our bodies will change and go through changes.

These are the times when you must depend on God to help you as well as trusting God to help your mate. There will be moments when your love for your mate will be tested. Live knowing that your mate's love is being tested as well. Get out of the middle, with your thoughts and plans, but get in the middle of God's grace and strength, to help both to walk through the difficult times. Labor to trust God to love when the strength of love is not sensed. Let your relationship with God keep you cognizant of the needs of your mate. Just because you are experiencing a difficult moment does not alleviate the needs of your mate. If you, husband, or wife is not concerned about pleasing the God-given needs of your mate you are displeasing and disobeying God.

> *"speaking to one another in psalms and hymns and spiritual songs, singing and making melody in your heart to the Lord, giving thanks always for all things to God the Father in the name of our Lord Jesus Christ, submitting to one another in the fear of God"* (Ephesians 5:19–21).

MENOPAUSE

Never view or use menopause as an excuse to neglect or present unpleasant behavior, nor for your husband to use as an excuse to have pleasure is another form, but a project or battle to conquer and win. In so doing, God has promised a gold medal even before the race is run.

From goodreads, Matthew Henry said:

> "Eve was not taken out of Adam's head to be on top of him, neither out of his feet to be trampled on by him, but out of his side to be equal with him, under his arm to be protected by him, and near his heart to be loved by him."

The Christian woman going through menopause does not need to feel helpless or alone. We are known intimately by God, and He cares for us.

*"Because you have made the Lord, who is my refuge,
Even the Most High, your dwelling place, -- No evil
shall befall you, Nor shall any plague come near your
dwelling; -- For He shall give His angels charge over
you, To keep you in all your ways"* (Psalm 91:9–11).

I want to emphasis that the Psalmist said, "in all your ways". Just reading the Word of God will not help unless you consciously and willingly say to yourself, I will do this and allow the Word of God to help me in every circumstance of my life. *"casting all your care upon Him, for He cares for you"* (1 Peter 5:7).

The woman of God who has determined to win knows that even after becoming knowledgeable of the Word of God, it is not an automatic behavior of obedience. It must be learned and applied. It is wisdom to use anything that is suffered to teach and learn a greater dimension in God. The woman of God who has learned that the Word of God is her help, survival, and strength will walk through menopause with greater ease and victory than an average woman.

*"though He was a Son, yet He learned obedience by the
things which He suffered"*. (Hebrews 5:8).

If you are married, you cannot expect the Word of God to work for you if you leave your husband out of the equation. The Word of God says you and your husband are one. You cannot expect God's Word to work for you when there is a violation of other parts. With all your anxieties and fears, cast them on Him for He cares for you. Yet, God wants you to honor all of His Word, not just the words that comfort you but those that challenge you as well. The Word of God says, "Husbands, love your wives, just as Christ also loved the church and gave Himself for her" (Ephesians 5:25). The Word of God also says, "Therefore, just as the church is subject to Christ, so let the wives be to their own husbands in everything" (Ephesians 5:24). Know that all the words of God are a word, a person. How can you divide a person?

When the Apostle Paul wrote to the Corinthian church, in I Cor 1:10-17, he addressed the division among the members. Some declared "I am of Paul", others declared they are of Apollos, Cephas, and Christ. They were declaring who they were following and honoring. Paul cleared up the matter with a question and a statement. "Is Christ divided?" Paul explained, it is the gospel of the cross and baptism in His Name that is the central word of all our beliefs and following. To honor and obey one part of God's Word and not the other is an attempt to divide the Person of Jesus Christ. How can you expect God to help, during your moment in life with menopause if you have ignored or neglect your husband?

Just as God has promised you, His grace is sufficient and His power is made perfect in weakness, if you are married, He has ordained the position of husband to help and assist the wife. Yes, it is true, your husband may not know anything about menopause or understand what you are going through, but if you trust God, He will help him to assist you through menopause. During these segments of your life, you must rely on and refresh yourself with your relationship with God as we discussed in chapter 1. The woman's body can be affected by the loss of estrogen and testosterone during menopause. Anything that lowers blood flow can impact the comfort of normal sexual activity. As the wife is going through menopause, the godly husband must always make it his business to encourage her, be patient with her, and always be attentive to her. His prayers will be noticed, and his reassurance will comfort his wife. Yes, his patience will be tested, and the loving wife can help him. Along with the patience a husband needs during this period, the wife must keep in mind and understanding that his sexual needs do not diminish just because there is not any sexual interest with her. Do not let a selfish spirit birth during menopause. A selfish spirit will put love on a shelf.

It is not that the wife doesn't love her husband, but she is dealing with an adjustment she feels should be excused because of something normal for a woman to go through, while there are things that are not normally affecting her.

Because it is scripturally advised to never deny your mate sex, unless for an agreed time of fasting, you must find the strength to openly discuss ways of sexual satisfaction when penetration is too painful. If the wife is a graduate from the class of chapter 5, neither the husband nor the wife's sexual relationship will have to experience total neglect. Let it be worship, not as a duty or a demand.

Remember,

> "Marriage is honorable among all, and the bed undefiled" (Hebrews 13:4).

During this time when the wife's mind and body are less sensitive to touching and fondling, words of love and affirmation are what she desperately needs. Her love for her husband can then respond to his need. The husband's love for his wife will demand him to keep a balance in the marriage with patience and understanding as well. Husbands, during this time in your wife's life, your sexual needs should never be demanded, but you must be truthful if asked. The husband must repeatedly remind himself of his wife's love for him and trust God that He will minister to his wife his need without ever demanding sexual activity. Trust God with ALL your heart and do not lean, trust, or depend on your understanding of what you see, hear, or experience.

During this time of your wife's life, your presence is needed even when it appears it is not wanted. It is being available and present but not constantly in her presence. As your wife goes through this moment, remember it is just a moment. The godly husband will trust God to keep him as well as being an encouragement to his wife, demonstrating patience and love when her behavior is strange, and emotions are soaring.

God has promised to all who love Him. Let Him be your refuge and strength. And take comfort in knowing that this too will pass. Knowing He has promised to keep you in all your ways.

> *"For he will order his angels to protect you in all you do"* (Psalms 91:11, Net)

God made the body, and He knows what He designed it to go through. Do not let menopause be an excuse and take advantage of feeling disorderly to act disorderly. This is a time for the husband and wife to purpose a greater time to pray together and commit the never experienced unexplained emotions, feelings, and body signals to the guidance and care of the Holy Spirit. When the wife knows that her husband is committed to her as she walks through this physical and functional change of her body, it will rob Satan of his plans to cause the wife to feel insecure and ignored. Remember, if God designed the body, He has a designed answer for the moment. "It is a change in life, not a change of life". <u>You will get your wife back.</u>

ERECTILE DYSFUNCTION (ED)

If you as a couple have reverenced and praised God in your sexual activity, the husband's level of erectile dysfunction (ED) will not be affected as others. God will honor your diligence of steadfastness in keeping your sexual life together, holy and honorable with each other in God. One of the greatest gifts God gave to mankind (male and female) is the power of words. As we believe what we say (negative or positive) those words make us who we are. We have heard and many say and believe:

"as he thinketh in his heart so is he"
"I am what I say I am"
"I have what I say I can have"
"I can be what I say I can be"
"he shall have whatsoever he saith"
"greater is He that is in me than he that is in the world"
"no weapon form against me shall prosper"
"I am who God says I am"
"whatever we ask, we know that we have the petitions"
"whatever things you ask when you pray, believe that you receive them"

What you are saying can make a major difference in your bodily reactions. Question: What would be your expressions if God, in His grace and love toward you, would pay off your home or one of your largest financial obligations? I suppose and yet I would say, "Thank you!, Hallelujah!, God I Praise You!" or just simply, "Praise God!" Or what would you say to God for something He would do for you? The relieving you of a throbbing headache, the generosity of a glorious peaceful day, or just the knowledge of His love? Maybe in your prayer time of asking Him for something dear to you, you would have absolutely zero hesitations or reservations to say or ask with the maximum of expressions.

I must remind you, that God gave sex to the husband and wife, and that "marriage is honorable, and the bed is undefiled". Just as you thank God for other things, what is wrong to thank Him for wonderful, fulfilling, and enjoyable intimate moments with your mate. You should never have any reservations or timidity in expressing to your mate and unto God referencing thoughts, ideas, or expressions of thanks to each other and God. Your words are powerful, limitless, and living. Your greatest source of remedy to menopause and ED are words and especially words from the wife's mouth. As husband and wife, just as you intensely discuss the purchasing of a new car, the remodeling of your home and its appearance and design. During the process, you discuss all the details of design, colors, the time involved, and what it would mean for the beauty of your home.

Just as your discussion and planning of other matters in life, it should be just as important to you of that special moment. It should be given the same intense attention. One problem with ED is the planning for gratification without the husband and wife having an open and detailed discussions of a prior fulfilling sexual moment. You should never underestimate the power of words. Words has the power to cause the mind to relive an event or an occasion of great value to you. The memory of your last enjoyable sexual experience, that is embedded in the mind, begins to attack the ED problem of the body. When husbands and wives openly discuss every aspect and detail of their sexual encounters, it will birth a closer and trusting relationship. The discussions will always produce a touching.

As a loving reminder, the Word of God says, "And they were both naked, the man and his wife, and were not ashamed" (Genesis 2:22). They were not ashamed before God nor each other. The Husband and wife should always be mindful of their physical and spiritual presentation. During the season of menopause and possible ED, the husband must take every opportunity to articulate appreciation and the wife must maintain a spirit of affirmation. While working together the spirit of God will incite loving utterances that will preserve a harmonious atmosphere.

Women are intimately appreciative
of verbal expressions (sensual)

Men are intimately appreciative of
bodily expressions (visual)

Men--, if you have begun experiencing moments of ED, you must trust your wife as you openly discuss it with her. When a man is already suffering from the initial state of ED, his immediate need is understanding and support from his wife. Sometimes the problem is associated with communication (language) and visual.

When the wife neglects her body, it adds to the ED problem of her husband. But when she begins to show signs of seriously working on her body to be fit for her husband, it slows down the ED attack. Remember, men are visual. It is wisdom for the wife to go beyond herself to see herself through the eyes of her husband and respond with the love she has for her husband and their marriage. As the wife lovingly shares her love and speaks explicitly the things she loves about their intimate moment and what she loves that her husband does that pleases her, this will help remedy the attack of ED greater than some medical sources. It is the power of words mixed with love.

DEPRESSION & ANXIETY

"Anxiety in the heart of man causes depression, but a good word makes it glad" (Proverbs 12:25).

Menopause and ED alone are difficult enough to cope with without adding depression or anxiety. Depression and anxiety are not only medical or mental problems, but they are mostly the problem of just being human, without trusting the Spirit of God. Neuroscience and psychology offer many theories and reasons, but none are mixed with faith. "Beloved, do not think it strange concerning the fiery trial which is to try you, as though some strange thing happened to you; 13 but rejoice to the extent that you partake of Christ's sufferings, that when His glory is revealed, you may also be glad with exceeding joy" (1 Peter 4:12-13).

THE WORD OF GOD IS LIVING

The Word is alive and can operate as a surgeon. The Word can go deeper than a surgeon can see and see things a microscope cannot reveal. The Word of God can uproot thoughts that have been planted by negative rendering embedded in the mind from the day you were born. When we put our lives in the hands of the living Word, we receive the redemptive work of Jesus Christ, the sustaining strength, and deliverance promised by the Holy Spirit. God never promised us a life without fiery trials. Just reading and memorizing God's Word will not give you your promised victories. *"For unto us was the gospel preached, as well as unto them: but the word preached did not profit them, not being mixed with faith in them that heard it"* (Hebrews 4:2). You must decide, just like any other decision you will make in life, I will not let how you feel decide what you do. Because of the rich love you have for each other, you can make an eternal decision, "I will do whatever it takes to have peace and harmony with my mate". You must let the Word living in you become the controlling factor of your life, not your emotions. Never say, "this is just too hard".

> *"Come to Me, all you who labor and are heavy laden, and I will give you rest. Take My yoke upon you and learn from Me, for I am gentle and lowly in heart, and you will find rest for your souls. For My yoke is easy and My burden is light"* (Matthew 11:28-30).

CHAPTER EIGHT

UN-MASKING DECEPTION

W HEN WE THINK of redemption, we think of new, something made over, paid off, recovery, or rescue. In a biblical understanding, we think of, deliverance, Atonement, free from guilt and salvation—that is, deliverance from sin. It is God's love, the power and the want, to do whatever it takes to provide for a person to move from a state of eternal destruction of being forever separated from God our creator to a constant fellowship with peace, love, joy, and supreme goodness with God our Father, Jesus Christ, and the Holy Spirit. After receiving the redemptive work of Jesus Christ, we begin to experience a love that is unexplainable. It is a love with a state of being without any inhibitions of constantly and always caring.

> *"For God so loved the world that He gave His only begotten Son, that whoever believes in Him should not perish but have everlasting life"* (John 3:16).

One day I was reading the Bible, as I try to do every day of my life, I was reading the gospel of John 3:16, and the Holy Spirit made me stop at the word "so". When He told me to stop, I did not understand why. I then began to look at definitions of the word. I looked at the Greek understanding of the word and the Greek word is houto {*hou'-to*} which means: *in this way or accordingly.* Still not understanding why I had to stop my reading, I then ask the Holy Spirit, "What are You trying to say to me?" He spoke to me and said, "The word "so" from My heart to your heart is to say, My love has no limits, My love has no ceiling and My love has no beginning and no end. Neither can you measure My love nor reach the end of My love. My love is not fragmented: nor can My love be altered or diminished in any fashion or form. There is no human capacity or mental qualities that can fully comprehend the purpose of or the explanation of My love. Yet, my love is consistent and will maintain a level of divine representation even when you are inconsistent in representing Me." "God so loved". His love goes on and on, never-ending and never-changing. True godly love does not have an element of controlling what is loved, but leave the one loved free to choose a position to accept or not to accept the provisions provided that you cannot control.

As I was reading the Word of God, I asked God on several occasions, "How was it so easy for Satan to deceive Eve?" Let us walk through the scriptures. As I was preparing to write this book, I read Genesis 1, 2, and 3 several times.

First, let's get into Eve's head. God made the tree, and it was beautiful, well-trimmed, and so pleasing to the sight of Eve, the woman. Women can see beauty in things the average man cannot see. It is natural for a woman to touch something that is appealing with a presentation of glory. Remember, God said Himself it was good. Can we agree with God and say everything

God made is good? The word good is not just to say good with the understanding of our everyday language. But "good" in the text is a Hebrew word, *"towb"* meaning merry, pleasant, desirable, and beautiful. When a woman is pleased with something and is pleasing to her sight, it is natural for her to have a desire to touch and care for it. I believe Satan was given the door to converse with Eve because of her attraction to the tree.

> *"And the Lord God commanded the man, saying, "Of every tree of the garden you may freely eat;—but of the tree of the knowledge of good and evil you shall not eat, for in the day that you eat of it you shall surely die"* (Genesis 2:16–17).

The first mistake of Adam and Eve—they never repeated what God said. Faith is never birth nor will it grow until God's Word is spoken and heard. *"So then faith comes by hearing and hearing by the Word of God"* (Romans 10:17). It does not come by words you say about the Word of God. When we do not say what God says, it robs us of the strength to obey God's Word. Satan said to Eve:

> *"Has God indeed said, 'You shall not eat of every tree of the garden'?"* (Genesis 3:1)

When Satan posed the question to Eve, it challenged her submission to Adam. When submission is not honored, a door of deception and independence opens. Eve's failure began when she failed to repeat what Adam, her husband, said. Deception begins within a person when their thoughts of selfish desires attach themselves to a spirit of independence.

> *"And the woman said to the serpent, "We may eat the*
> *fruit of the trees of the garden; but of the fruit of the*
> *tree which is <u>in the midst of the garden</u>, God has said,*
> *'You shall not eat it, <u>nor shall you touch it</u>, lest you*
> *die.""* (Genesis 3:2–3)

God gave us a warning in Deuteronomy 4:2, *"You shall not add to the word which I command you, nor take from it, that you may keep the commandments of the LORD your God which I command you"*. Faith cannot be birthed when adding or taking away from God's word. Eve's response violated Deuteronomy 4:2, she added to it and took away from it.

By the statement of Eve, I am convinced she visited the tree more than once before her encounter with Satan. Satan is a deceiver, and he will quickly respond to anyone who steps into themselves and outside of divine protection. Satan knows that the spirit of independence from authority leaves you open to believe an untruth that births rebellion. Rebellion is cruel. It will give you a sense of strong security until the goal of deception is completed. The deceived one is now open to believe any comprehensive lie.

> *"Then the serpent said to the woman, "You will not*
> *surely die. For God knows that in the day you eat of*
> *it your eyes will be opened, and you will be like God,*
> *knowing good and evil"* (Genesis 3:4–5).

It is difficult to detect a lie when you embellish the Word of God with manufactured truth. God never said, *"nor shall you touch it"*. Eve released a thought that did not have any governing authority from the author of truth, which left her mind unprotected. The same spirit of rebellion that was in Lucifer, was released within the words he spoke to Eve, a spirit of independence—operating without honoring authority. When you are not under authority, you cannot be protected by authority; the authority of God or the authority He has placed in your life.

When living and confronting issues of life, especially dealing with the Devil, a wife's safety is in submission to her husband. So many wives live with the misconception that submission is being ruled and subservient to her husband. Submission is putting a demand on God to minister to her husband for guidance, wisdom, protection, and instructions for their lives. Submission is a form of ministering and respecting the gift God has placed in the wife's life. As strange as it may sound, submission releases a higher level of love and gratification. When a wife truly submits to her husband, it puts a demand on God to impower her husband to cover her in every facet of living. God uses the Church to symbolize the meaning of submission and covering. How is this principle a truth with God and the Church, but not the husband and wife?

> *"For the husband is head of the wife, as also Christ is head of the church; and He is the Savior of the body"* (Ephesians 5:23).

Rebellion will drain you of the richness of sexual cohesiveness. Rebellion will cause a husband to question true love. Satan continuously attempts to destroy the divine cohesive relationship and fellowship of God and man as well as dismantle and destroy the unity, oneness, and fellowship of the inhabitance on earth.

We discussed how Eve was deceived, but for Adam to willfully receive the fruit and eat has baffled me for years. In my study and prayer time, I believe God has answered. God's love gave Adam a free will and His love gave him the best of life to enjoy. Let me see if I can paint a picture.

When God made Eve, knowing that God cannot do anything less than good, she was beyond any descriptive expressions of beauty. Her physical body was ineffable magnificent. Adam's contentment caused him to praise and thank God daily. Her ministering to Adam was almost parallel to God's love and ministering to him. So, without the foresight nor faith to believe for another Eve to be brought to him, he ate the fruit. In all that God will do for us because He is love, we must ourselves keep all things in perspective. Because He is God, He cannot help but to give us, whom He loves, the best of what He has to give. It is obvious that Adam put himself before God to have Eve for himself. The weakest moment of any man is the inability to be sober when facing a spirit of rebellion from the source of his gratification, his wife.

The question is so often asked; how can anything so good be so bad? When a man, especially a husband, does not labor in putting God first, he will not only let himself fall, but will cause a generation to blunder in life. Adam did not only fall himself, but all his seed fell. All mankind is now laboring to grasp the truths and concepts to understand the nature of God's intentions and plans.

HOW ARE YOU THINKING

The question is asked without verbalization, why would God make and give something as pleasurable, pleasing, and gratifying as the sexual experience yet with inhibitions and negative thinking embedded in the minds of so many believers?

When the origin and purpose of sex are not known, Satan will help you generate thoughts that are elusive, deceptive, and secretive, and sex becomes only pleasurable and gratifying. When pleasure is your only thought and purpose of sex, it is the deception that the devil has planted in the minds of our youth, young adults, and even some married couples.

Because this deception does not include a thankfulness to God and a purpose in giving to the mate love and pleasure as a service in worship, the heart is empty of glorification and filled with guilt. Why? Because sex is a gift from God and whenever a gift from God is not honored, guilt is always the result of the action. This guilt destroys the freedom and foresight of the necessity to teach our children God's plan and purpose of the sexuality of mankind. When something is hidden and treated as secretive to a young mind, it will ignite a spirit of curiosity and exploration, and will leave the mind darkened and void of truth. I believe this is the reason for St. Augustine's statement, "Sex is *sinful*,"

When the origin, purpose, plan, and reason for sex are taught biblically, there is a realm with God where we can be complete without any controlling needs of human sexual pleasure. It is that place where the needs of the body do not control our activity because of our fellowship with our Creator is fully linked to the revelation of Genesis 2:22, *"Then the rib which the Lord God had taken from man He made into a woman, and He brought her to the man."* The heart and mind will become devoted to God's heart and plan for the human body and sexuality. God did not intend to have any inhibitions or restrictions in marriage. It should be seen and honored as the love and goodness of God. We should be thankful for the un-restricted love of God's heart, never to be seen, viewed, or have any restrictions but as an order of life that is pleasing and satisfying to God in our fellowship with him.

I am convinced that the devil was doing all he could, not only to cause sin to come into our lives and separate us from God. He also attacked the glorious and wonderful gift God gave to husband and wife in their holy intimacy. What does the body being naked have to do with the forbidden fruit? Yes, they lost their innocence, but the nakedness with each other was not the problem; it was their nakedness before God. And they knew they were naked, but why was that more important to Adam than eating the forbidden fruit? When God said, *"Adam, where art thou?"* He said we hid because we were naked. God asked him, *"Have you eaten of the fruit from the tree of the knowledge of good and evil?"* I believe Satan knew that along with the entrance of sin and man falling from the dominion of the authority of earth, he had also attached the glorious gift of sex. Remember the Bible says in Genesis 2:25, *"They were naked and not ashamed."* I believe Adam and Eve spent eons together worshipping God while celebrating each other. When they came together sexually, pleasurably, pleasing, and gratifying, it was a oneness, a ministering to each other in worship to God that infuriated Satan. He witnessed Adam and Eve having a oneness beyond the oneness he had with God when he was created. It was a oneness Satan could never experience. That is why He is doing all He can to promote a continual perversion of something so beautiful.

CHAPTER NINE

REDEMPTIVE MEASURES

U NFORTUNATELY, WHEN IT comes to today's sexual revolution and its perversion, an incomplete gospel is being preached. It is a teaching of "kingdom blessings" without including the need for transformation. The teaching of kingdom blessing inclusive of transformation will equip the believer with the love and power to comply with scripture as well as receiving the blessings promised. The key statement is, **"The power of love."** The power of love will inspire transformation to bring us back to the original state of being before sinful habits and perversion.

> *"Therefore, if anyone is in Christ, he is a **new creation**; old things have passed away; behold, all things have become new"* (2 Corinthians 5:17).

> *"Likewise you also, reckon yourselves to be **dead indeed to sin**, but **alive to God in Christ Jesus our Lord**"* (Romans 6:11).

*"But **seek first the kingdom of God** and His righteousness, and **all these things shall be added** to you"* (Matthew 6:33).

To Capsulized it all:

"In Christ, the Holy Spirit is helping me to become a new creation. By the faith I am receiving from the Word of God, I am becoming dead indeed to sin and alive to God in Christ Jesus our Lord. I seek first, before anything else, the kingdom of God and everything I need will be added to me."

We must never forget that we are living after the fall and we live with the knowledge of good and evil. The Hebrew word for knowledge is *"da'at"* which means, skillful, ability, and discernment.

We are skillful with ability, yet with discernment to know that without the guidance of the Holy Spirit, we can't see the built-in manipulation weaved in the evil to destroy my future. When we disobey God, the only wisdom most believers have is to repent. Repentance means; to change one's mind that will inevitably change my behavior. It is not only to repent of an error but to move from the error. Once repentance is received and honored, all of God's wisdom is available. It is demented to ever think that we could be wise and knowledgeable enough to live without God's wisdom, guidance, and instructions. As we live in this age, we know that knowledge has power. The more knowledge we have in God and of God, *good* has the potential to rule. If we have more knowledge of the world without God, *evil* has the potential to rule. I say potential because our will must be properly informed to make the right choices. Our will is the only thing that God gave to us that is all ours. That is because God himself is love. The main attribute of love is to give everyone the allowance to make **the right** choices. Because of His love, God gave to man the will to choose. Love is the absolute deciding vote. In our new birth, the love of God lives in our newly created spirit. As that love is nurtured, matured, and lived, it invites us into the word of God where we are empowered by the Holy Spirit to live His life.

I am convinced that the greatest asset to obedience is not just say "no" but to teach all the benefits of a relationship with God. The mistakes that I made as a parent and many other parents have made is that we did not teach our children the purpose and plan of God for sex. I said to my children, as many other parents, NO, NO, NO, DON'T, DON'T, DON'T and how wrong it is to have children before marriage, while they were asking WHAT, and WHY. They accepted that it was wrong because of the love of their parents, but they wanted to ask, "why am I having these feelings and urges, what should I do with them, and how am I to handle them?" Youth, young adults, and adults did understand, that there is a proper time and proper order, but did not have or understand the spiritual relevance of God's intension and purpose. We did understand "do not". But the words, "do not" wasn't the strength and spiritual revelation needed to empower the will to say, "I will not".

I remember growing up in my home as a young boy, it was not even allowed to ask questions about sex. We were told to leave it alone until marriage, yet there were not any explanations about the body's reactions and behaviors in normal everyday functioning. If all youth were like me, we were having feelings, body reactions, and thoughts we felt guilty of not knowing it was the normality of the body. There was not any teaching or explanations just "NO," "DON'T," "YOU CAN'T," and "JUST WAIT TILL YOU GET MARRIED." I know now not to blame my parents and the adults responsible for my growing up. It is not possible to teach what was not taught and not permitted to engage in learning.

God knows our bodies better than we do. Remember He made the body and gave to the body its appetites and desires before the fall of man in Genesis 3. When the gospel of transformation is taught from birth to marriage, one truth that is known and respected is:

> *"Or do you not know that your body is the temple of the Holy Spirit who is in you, whom you have from God, and you are not your own? For you were bought at a price; therefore, **glorify** God in your body and in your spirit, which is God's"* (1 Corinthians 6:19–20)

We have taught so much on the body as the temple of the Holy Spirit and that the body belongs to God, but we have not explained how to glorify God in our bodies as well as our spirit, which is also God's. Glorifying God in our body is not just praise and a shout. It is inclusive of the functioning of the body as well.

RULES WITHOUT EXPLANATIONS LEAVE
THE MIND OPEN TO CURIOSITY

We do not give a newborn meat, and we have explained that. We do not let a ten-year-old child drive a vehicle, and we have explained that. We do not let a child handle a firearm, and we have explained that. We do not expect a twelve-year-old child to pass a college exam and we understand that. But we tell our young boys and girls to not have sex, but do not explain why. The only explanation that was primarily taught was, "Don't have children before marriage", but the major topics and teaching were never biblically taught. Abstinence was taught, but the strength, power, and purpose to maintain abstinence were left out of the equation. Abstinence is spiritual, not natural, and cannot be properly honored except by scriptural articulations and application. Just saying "NO" is not the answer. Just to say no without having a conviction and understanding for the purpose and origin of sex will birth a constant questioning and frustration in the mind of our youth and unmarried adults. Because of the discussed pleasure of sex, they will surrender to sexual behavior without examining any unwanted implications that could develop.

It is time for parents, Sunday school teachers, and the five-fold ministries to stop, take a breath, and first, teach ourselves the meaning and purpose of the sexual union. The first thing we must learn and teach is that it is a <u>sexual union,</u> not just sex. It is not only a sexual union of husband and wife but a glorification of God in the sexual union. That should only have ministered in the marital union. We must learn and teach that first:

A. The body was made by God and for God, and all forms of functions to please God.
B. Sex is a gift from God.
C. Sex is given only to the marital union.
D. Sex is given for four purposes:

1. Establishing a blood covenant between husband and wife, with God.
2. A worship to God while thanking God for the gift and pleasure of sex in the marital union.
3. The ultimate expression of Godly love & pleasure between husband and wife.
4. Propagating the human race.

The parents, Sunday School teachers, and the five-fold ministry must have the faith as to how this tender and delicate subject can be taught to our youth and young adults. We must trust the Holy Spirit to assimilate these truths that must be taught to them and believe that these truths build a resilience to say "no" with a respect to God and will abstain until marriage. If the godly beauty, love, purpose, and God's involvement in the sexual union is not taught as a gift from God to the marital union, it carries a negative impulse.

That is why the mind of men, such as St. Augustine, equated sex to be a deterrent to spiritual living. Timothy's testimony must become a reality in the functioning of kingdom transformation.

> *"But you must continue in the things which you have*
> *learned and been assured of, knowing from whom you*
> *have learned them, and that **from childhood** you have*

known the Holy Scriptures, which are able to make you wise for salvation through faith which is in Christ Jesus" (2 Timothy 3:14–15).

The only way this sexual revolution and perversion can begin to decline is to follow this simple principle. ***"and that from childhood you have known the Holy Scriptures."***

One day I said to a young boy in my church, "two plus two is not four," and he looked at me with a strange and confused expression and replied, "What do you mean Pastor?" I said again, "two plus two is not four, "He then said to me with full assurance and confidence, "two plus two is four Pastor". I then asked him, "how can you be so sure of that?" His response surprised me, "It is in my school-book and that is all I have heard, and it has not changed". Just like that, the young lad stood on what he had learned from his books and continuous of hearing, I could not change his mind. If the biblical purpose and plan for sex are taught to our children, until it becomes ingrained in their minds just like the young lad in my church many lives could be changed and saved. As these truths are taught in the homes from birth to marriage and reiterated in church group functions, the will to honor our Creator and respect His created and purchased body would live in the hearts of the believers. Sex could be comfortably taught to our children that it is holy and God-given. Teaching that the body is God's property and how to respect Him with the body. Teaching that sex is holy and should be fully enjoyed and experienced in marriage.

As we teach our children, young adults and unmarried to love God and to receive Him, His love will empower their will to will to please Him. Sex should not be labeled as a restriction but, freely given in marriage. Only God's love can empower a life of abstinence till marriage.

> *"But **put on** the Lord Jesus Christ, and make no provision for the flesh, to fulfill its lusts"* (Romans 13:14).

To "put on" the Lord Jesus Christ is a daily activity of, saying, and repeating the Word of God to ourselves in all facets and techniques of communicating. It is truly becoming what you want to be by using the power of God's word to shape character and behavior.

> *"For assuredly, I say to you, whoever says to this mountain, 'Be removed and be cast into the sea,' and does not doubt in his heart, but believes that those things he says will be done, <u>he will have whatever he says</u>".* (Mark 11:23)

I do not fault our youth and even unmarried adults only for the aggressive sexual behavior and perversion that our nation is experiencing. I include Bible teachers, fathers, and mothers who had limited understanding and were not biblically knowledgeable of the subject. So, we could not teach children the truth about something incredibly special to God and a gift to man and woman in marriage. If most homes were like the home I grew up in, sex was not discussed and if we had any questions, we were instructed to be quiet and told it should not be talked about. It was ignorance on the part of parents, and the church. To not discuss a subject, leaves an open door to conceive an incorrect precept and conclusion. Parents and biblical teachers should be honest and say,

> Yes, it is gratifying, but God purposes it only in marriage. In marriage, there is not any guilt or a violation of the body that belongs to God. Yes, we, Daddy and Mother enjoy each other, and it is an honor to God that husbands and wives give themselves to each other. *"Let the husband render to his wife the affection due her, and likewise also the wife to her husband"*. (1 Corinthians 7:3) But outside of marriage, it is a damnable thing and is called fornication. *"Nevertheless, because of sexual immorality, let each man have his own wife, and let each woman have her own husband"* (1Corinthians 7:2).

Many parents and bible teachers avoided the subject of sex because of being so ambiguous about the subject themselves. And to add to the problem, man's own will to progress, to achieve, and to pursue success in selfish decisions; Changed God's prescribed formula of life and living to one that fits society and culture. Society is saying to youth and young adults to make plans to live by obtaining sufficient education to qualify for suitable employment and protect yourself from pregnancy or getting someone pregnant. Shamefully said, having God as the primary source for life and successful living is not primary anymore. When the Word of God is the primary focus for teaching life and living, nothing will become a separate part of living as sex has become in the lives of youth and the unmarried. Abstinence is not viewed as a choice or even a possibility. When the mind and the spirit grow up together in spiritual knowledge and understanding, there is a power and strength built within the believer that will have the ability to withstand temptations and limit the perversion that has been propagated in our society and this world. The covenant of marriage is not only a vow of husband and wife to each other, but the greater sense of covenant is the blood covenant. The blood covenant between husband and wife is not even discussed in most of our homes and churches. It may be right to say, "in none of our homes and churches. The purpose of the Husband, not boyfriend, to be the one to break his wife's, not girlfriend, hymen is to establish a blood covenant between the two. And, of course, only a virgin has an unbroken hymen. God made the body and placed the hymen in the woman's vaginal opening for this reason.

It is intended by God for the husband to be the one to break his wife's hymen. It was a breaking to form a bond. God Himself established the truth – there is no covenant without blood. When the membrane (hymen) is broken blood is released. What is not taught and should be taught in every home and every youth and young adults church meeting is that when the membrane is broken, God purposed it for a spiritual bonding to take place. A supernatural process of mending, blending, tying, and building a lasting bond in the woman's (wife's) heart to the man (husband) being the first to enter and break the hymen membrane. It is the Spirit of God working behind the scenes. The membrane has no other purpose but to release blood to seal and bond the marital vows and union. If our youth and young adult knew and understood this godly principle and structure, there would be fewer divorces and more virgins in our society.

I strongly urge every God-fearing parent and church leaders to bring back to the family the teaching of the oneness with God, to teach, *"He is before all things, and in Him, all things consist. And He is the head of the body, the church, who is the beginning, the firstborn from the dead, that in all things He may have the preeminence"* (Colossians 1:17-18). To reference, *"He is the first of all things."* When God is first in all that we are, all things that He has given to us can be a praise and worship to Him.

> *"that in the dispensation of the fullness of the times He might gather together in one all things in Christ, both which are in heaven and which are on earth—in Him.* ***11*** *In Him also we have obtained an inheritance, being predestined according to the purpose of Him who works all things according to the counsel of His will"*, (Ephesians 1:10–11)

As soon as children can understand words and have the ability to communicate thoughts with questions and concerns, this is the perfect time to teach and train their young minds that their bodies are made and treasured by God and that sex is a gift from God to be honored in marriage. The more a statement of truth is spoken and heard, the more power is infused within the mind to live the life of that truth. A parent asked me in one of our church meetings, "At what age should parents begin to teach our children about their body and sex?" I answered, "At the age of their first question. It doesn't matter if it is a question based on curiosity, a repeating of what was heard, or a thought from a pure heart". Keep in mind, if you do not tell and teach them, they are going to ask someone else, and most likely, they will get the wrong source or information. There is a serious need for godly parents and teachers to properly assimilate and communicate such sensitive information. We must teach them that sex is holy and given by God, to the marriage, and should be preserved for that glorious time. It must be taught that only in the marriage, they would be able to express back to God a praise of thanks as they give their bodies to each other. First, knowing they have pleased God and then experience God's expression of His love in their activities as husband and wife. I believe with all my heart it would slow down the aggressive sexual environment that is among our unmarried youth, high school students, college individuals, and single adults when realized it is holy unto God and can only be reverenced in a marriage. The body of Christ must know and teach that sex is a highly exalted activity rather than just simply fun and pleasurable. Everyone must understand the nature of the omnipresence of God. If sex is experienced before marriage, God is violated. He is forced to observe and witness an unholy and an ungodly function.

As a believer, God lives in you, and He did not leave you while you were involved in any activities that God only purposed for marriage between a husband and wife. It is conducive that all teaching and training departments of our churches boldly begin to teach the truth about the body God made. God made the body to have sexual desires and was purposed to experience pleasure and gratification as the human race is propagated. I will end by saying, "If sex were not an experience of love, pleasure and gratification, the human race would be millions less than what there is today".

"Marriage is honourable in all, and the bed undefiled: but whoremongers and adulterers God will judge" (Hebrews 13:4).

"God is love and God loves to be loved. He loves to love others through you as His love is expressed from you by His love in you".

CONCLUSION

Yes, it is true. To grow spiritually is to study and receive the truth that is in the Word of God. To learn to hear the voice of God and to be led by the Holy Spirit is invaluable to the Christian (the believer). Yet, one of the most infused and troubled parts of mankind that has infected the local church and society is the sexual revolution. This sexual revolution is among the singles, divorcees, among the clergy, and the married with other married individuals. I am convinced that because the church did not have the proper understanding, or maybe I should say, the right revelation from God about sex, we were left alone to its pleasure. Yes, the bible is clear.

> **"You have heard that it was said to those of old, 'You shall not commit adultery.' But I say to you that whoever looks at a woman to lust for her has already committed adultery with her in his heart"** (Matthew 5:27–28).

> *"Foods for the stomach and the stomach for foods, but God will destroy both it and them. Now the body is not for sexual immorality but for the Lord, and the Lord for the body"* (1 Corinthians 6:13).

But when there is not a clear understanding of God's purpose for intimacy, abuse will happen. When participating in a perverted state of sexuality, pleasure becomes the only purpose of sexual engagement. This is the reason the spirit of man cannot experience the joy that God can give. When Godly joy is absent, the peace of God cannot honor gratification and will leave the heart empty of glorification but filled with guilt.

Parents and church leaders are reticent about teaching God's plan for sex in the marital relationship and how to honor Him. The church and parents have taught "no" and "do not" very successfully while the world has taken and amplified sexual pleasure and gratification successfully. When the pleasure of sex is the only thing experienced, it is extremely difficult for our children and the unmarried adults to simply just say "no". It requires the perpetual teaching of the Word of God to generate the power necessary to honor God and His principles. ¬The power, authority, and strength we receive from His word will structure and restructure your thoughts toward God and His purpose to keep you focused on remaining pure until marriage. The bible says to us in Nehemiah 8:10 "for the joy of the Lord is your strength". The joy of God being pleased leaves us with an unexplainable joy that surpasses the mind of the natural man.

The thoughts and wisdom from the mind of man without the Word of God leaves mankind absent of strength to maintain purity until marriage. The Word of God has an internal agent, known as the Person of the Holy Spirit, who will teach us, guide us, and keep us.

"But the Helper, the Holy Spirit, whom the Father will send in My name, He will teach you all things,

and bring to your remembrance all things that I said to you" (John 14:26).

It is the power of God's Word that can and will keep us in all things and matters of life. In Hebrew 4:12, It is the Word of God that is living and powerful. It is the Word of God that is sharper than any two-edged sword, piercing even to the division of soul and spirit and of joints and marrow. It is the Word of God who is a discerner of the thoughts and intents of the heart. As we believe and speak the Word of God to ourselves, we can move every mountain of perversion that Satan attempts to use to destroy God's plan of pure joy and happiness in relationships.

"For assuredly, I say to you, whoever says to this mountain, 'Be removed and be cast into the sea,' and does not doubt in his heart, but believes that those things he says will be done, he will have whatever he says" (Mark 11:23).

Happiness and Joy is a LIFE of faith:
It is an action of following all truth that is
understood, (OBEDIENCE) and a decision to do
all that is revealed, (RELATIONSHIP).

After reading this book, I pray you have heard and received the purpose of God in all He has given to mankind. If you have not asked Jesus Christ into your life to have a relationship with him, I pray you will do that now. Having a life in Him and with Him, there is "nothing missing and nothing lacking".